# MASTER YOUR DISASTER

A Readiness, Response, and Recovery Guide

## Leann Hackman-Carty

Copyright © 2017 by Leann Hackman-Carty, HackmanCarty & Associates

All rights reserved.

No part of this book may be reproduced, scanned, or distributed in any printed or electronic form without permission.

First Edition: December 2017

Printed in the United States of America

Business ISBN: 9781704915913

Library of Congress Control Number: 2017917539

CreateSpace Independent Publishing Platform, North Charleston, SC

www.MasterYourDisaster.ca

# ABOUT THE BOOK

Natural disasters are happening everywhere. Earthquakes, hurricanes, and man-made perils have left communities anxious and confused about their own emergency preparedness. In this unique guide, preparedness and recovery expert Leann Hackman-Carty shows you how to prepare your business for a number of devastating scenarios. Gleaned from years of experience with disaster recovery organizations, her specialized insight will help you understand the different levels of disaster preparation and recovery.

Hackman-Carty discusses how to:
- understand the types and phases of a disaster,
- identify available resources at your office,
- assemble an emergency business supply kit,
- know when to activate your plan and evacuate,
- keep your employees safe,
- identify critical business functions,
- create a business continuity plan,
- communicate with your employees, suppliers, and customers,
- use local, regional and federal programs as resources, and
- stop a natural disaster from catching you off guard.

No one knows what tomorrow holds, but Hackman-Carty's advice can help you prepare for the worst. Master Your Disaster (Business Edition) gives you the confidence to act calmly and efficiently when the time comes. Your new foundation in emergency preparedness, response, and recovery will make the chaos more controllable—and survivable.

# TESTIMONIALS

*As the former head of the New Zealand Aid Program, managing disasters across the Pacific during cyclone season was an integral and critical dimension of my role. The information in this book is invaluable. With the rapid increase in natural disasters and severe weather events in recent years, disaster preparedness and planning is absolutely essential for individuals, communities and for businesses to mitigate risk, loss of life and cost. If only Leann Hackman-Carty's book had been compulsory reading before New Zealand's big earthquake hit Christchurch in 2011!*

**Amanda Ellis, Special Advisor to the President, East-West Center (Hawaii, USA), former Ambassador to the UN (Geneva, Switzerland), and Deputy Secretary International Development New Zealand Ministry of Foreign Affairs and Trade**

*The content in these guidebooks is invaluable to prepare businesses for a disaster. On a global scale we have witnessed the significant impact of disasters on businesses and communities. Being prepared for various risks is a smart thing for a business to do if it wants to have continuity of operations.*

**Barb Mowat, Small Business Expert & Founder of GroYourBiz (Vancouver, Canada)**

*No business should be without a copy! In the Business Edition of Master Your Disaster, Ms. Hackman-Carty not only explains why you should have a method to handle any disaster, but also explains some of the economics of not being in business after a disaster. A great read for all businesses.*

**Howard Pierpont, Americas Business Continuity Coach, DERA Institute for Preparedness and Resilience (Greeley, USA)**

*Leann's guidebooks on disaster recovery could not be more relevant or timely. Hurricanes, tornadoes, tsunami's, earthquakes, monsoons, floods and fires make us all vulnerable since we don't know when they're going to happen, or the devastation they will leave behind. Preparedness is not an option but a necessity. Finding a way forward must be done. Whether it is short-term rebuilding or long-term recovery, we need to have a plan in place.*

*Leann's guidebooks provide practical templates to help individuals, businesses and communities face less traumatic impacts by having a plan in place, and the necessary confidence to act.*

*Having partnered with Leann on a manmade disaster in the past, the impact of designer drugs on Native American's in the United States and Canada, I not only endorse her guidebooks for Canada but will personally recommend them to the seven public interest groups in the United States that represent states, cities, counties, regional communities and tribal governments. We must do better!*

**Loretta Avent, Former Deputy Assistant to President Clinton for Intergovernmental Affairs, White House Liaison to Indian Country and Liaison to First Lady Hillary Rodham Clinton's Office**

# ACKNOWLEDGEMENTS

It truly does take a village to raise a child.

I am grateful to my own village of family, friends and colleagues that have supported my personal and professional growth over the years.

A special thanks to my former boss Al Duerr, Mayor of Calgary (1989-2001) who mentored me during the early part of my career. He taught me the importance of leading with integrity, even when it wasn't the easiest road on which to travel. He modelled an inclusive, servant style of leadership that encouraged widespread grassroots civic participation, and often said that ultimately a community would be judged by how it treated its most vulnerable citizens.

I also want to acknowledge Jeff Finkle, President and CEO of the International Economic Development Council (IEDC) and his staff at Restore Your Economy. Their consistent support, encouragement, and advice over the past decade have nurtured my professional growth and personal desire to make an impact in the emerging area of business and economic recovery.

I also want to recognize the Canadian Red Cross for its willingness to develop and implement innovative business and economic recovery programs. Their growing commitment to addressing the area of livelihoods is making a significant difference in the communities they serve.

Finally, a big thank you to my sister Deidre, for helping design the book covers. Your ongoing support and encouragement are greatly appreciated.

This *Master Your Disaster* series of guidebooks is dedicated to my immediate family Graham, Jordan, and Sage. Thank you for letting me spend long nights and early mornings at my computer completing this manuscript.

In the words of the late author and poet Maya Angelou:

> "I've learned that no matter what happens, or how bad it seems today, life does go on, and it will be better tomorrow. I've learned that you can tell a lot about a person by the way he/she handles these three things: a rainy day, lost luggage, and tangled Christmas tree lights. I've learned that regardless of your relationship with your parents, you'll miss them when they're gone from your life. I've learned that making a "living" is not the same thing as making a "life." I've learned that life sometimes gives you a second chance. I've learned that you shouldn't go through life with a catcher's mitt on both hands; you need to be able to throw something back. I've learned that whenever I decide something with an open heart, I usually make the right decision. I've learned that even when I have pains, I don't have to be one. I've learned that every day you should reach out and touch someone. People love a warm hug, or just a friendly pat on the back. I've learned that I still have a lot to learn. I've learned that people will forget what you said, people will forget what you did, but people will never forget how you made them feel."

As you go through this guidebook and complete the template, may you be inspired and empowered to meet your own challenges with boldness, and design a more resilient tomorrow for your business.

# TABLE OF CONTENTS

| | |
|---|---|
| **ABOUT THE BOOK** | III |
| **TESTIMONIALS** | IV |
| **ACKNOWLEDGEMENTS** | VI |
| **TABLE OF CONTENTS** | VIII |
| **PREFACE** | X |
| **BACKGROUND** | 1 |
|     EMERGENCY VS. DISASTER | 1 |
|     TYPES OF DISASTERS | 4 |
|         *Natural disasters* | 4 |
|         *Manmade and technological disasters* | 5 |
|     COST OF DISASTERS | 6 |
|     NATURE OF DISASTERS | 8 |
|     PHASES OF A DISASTER | 9 |
|         *Prevention and Mitigation* | 10 |
|         *Preparedness* | 11 |
|         *Response* | 12 |
|         *Recovery* | 12 |
| **BUSINESS MODULE** | 16 |
|     ASSESS AND MITIGATE YOUR RISKS | 18 |
|         *Identify critical business functions* | 19 |
|         *Understand your insurance plan* | 20 |
|     PLAN AND PRACTICE YOUR RESPONSE | 21 |
|         *Assemble an emergency business supply kit* | 22 |
|         *Develop evacuation procedures and identify routes* | 23 |
|         *Identify an alternate office location* | 23 |
|         *Consider employees* | 24 |
|         *Ensure important records are safe* | 25 |
|         *Identify critical business processes* | 28 |
|         *Rank critical business processes* | 29 |
|         *Develop strategies to address risks* | 29 |
|         *Create a crisis communication plan* | 30 |
|     ACTIVATE YOUR BUSINESS CONTINUITY PLAN | 31 |
|     RECOVER FROM THE INCIDENT | 32 |
|     UPDATE YOUR PLAN | 32 |
|     TEMPLATE #1: STAND APART© BUSINESS CONTINUITY PLAN | 33 |

## **CONCLUSION** **43**
### About the author 45
### Table of figures 46
### References 47

# PREFACE

Every part of the planet is vulnerable to disasters, whether they are natural-occurring events such as floods, fires, earthquakes, and hurricanes or manmade disasters such as terrorism, chemical spills, or nuclear accidents. Not only have disasters become more frequent in recent years, their impacts have also become more costly.

Unfortunately disasters often strike with little or no warning. The damage they inflict can be in the billions of dollars. Individuals, businesses, and communities can face dramatic social and humanitarian consequences in the wake of a disaster, as well as sudden economic losses and dislocation.

Disasters expose people and communities to vulnerabilities they didn't know they had. By spending time preparing, mitigating, and preventing disasters, individuals, businesses, and communities will be better able to respond, recover, and remain more resilient in the face of disruptive change.

I have dedicated my entire career to working with communities. During the early part of my career, I spent over a decade working as the mayor of Calgary's Executive Assistant for Community and Economic Development. After that, I continued to work in that field by running a provincial association for economic development professionals while continuing to consult privately in the field.

I must admit that I fell into the business and economic disaster recovery field quite by accident. In 2013, as floodwaters in the southern part of my province continued to rise and devastate communities, I started work in what would become an increasingly important part of my personal and professional life.

In 2016, as wildfires began to consume the area surrounding Fort McMurray, my alarm went off again. This time, I spent over a year on business and economic recovery efforts.

In 2017, I began teaching communities about economic recovery and resiliency concepts to help them better prepare and recover from disasters. Each time I train, I feel honored to have been able to share, equip, and empower more individuals, businesses, and communities in this area. While it is usually just a first step, it is an important one.

As I watch the news every day, I am increasingly convinced that, if we are to make a real difference in how we as individuals, businesses, and communities respond and recover from disasters, there has to be a better way. We can't keep doing the same thing over and over again. It isn't working.

I am a firm believer that the more tools, information, and resources that individuals, businesses, and communities have access to, the more empowered they will be to take charge of their own response and recovery efforts.

As global citizens, we all need to be more prepared in this area. It could mean the difference between saving our life, keeping our livelihood, and maintaining our quality of life. Governments, emergency response organizations, and humanitarian relief agencies cannot do it alone. We must act now.

I have designed this guidebook to be an easy, practical way for you to Stand **APART**© by:
- ✓ Assessing and mitigating your risk
- ✓ Planning and practicing your response
- ✓ Activating your plan
- ✓ Recovering successfully from the incident
- ✓ Templating your activity in an easy to use format

Purchasing this book is your first step. Templating your activity should be next.

I encourage you in your efforts to become more aware and empowered in this area. In doing so, you will be able to find hope in the face of hopelessness. Take control of your destiny. Have your plan in place, so you can *Master Your Disaster*.

# BACKGROUND

## EMERGENCY VS. DISASTER

In the framework of response and recovery, there is a difference between the terms *emergency* and *disaster*.[1]

An *emergency* is an event that can be responded to by using resources available at hand, implying there is no need to request external assistance. First responders in our communities attend to these events on a routine basis. The majority of emergencies is handled locally or at the provincial or state level and do not require direct federal involvement.

A *disaster* overwhelms the capacity of local responders and requires additional resources not readily available locally. They often result in serious harm to the safety, health, and welfare of residents and can include widespread damage to property. The combination of hazards, vulnerability, and inability to reduce the potential negative consequences of risk results in disaster.[2]

When an event overwhelms the ability of a local government to respond, they will often appeal to the province or state for additional assistance. In some instances, they will declare a national calamity as a way to request additional international humanitarian assistance and support to help cope with the overwhelming impact of the disaster.

Figure 1[3] provides a side-by-side comparison of the two concepts.

Figure 1. *Emergencies vs. Disasters*

| Emergencies | Disasters |
| --- | --- |
| Interaction with familiar faces | Interaction with unfamiliar faces |
| Familiar tasks and procedures | Unfamiliar tasks and procedures |
| Intra-organizational coordination needed | Intra- and inter-organizational coordination needed |
| Roads, telephones and facilities intact | Road may be blocked or jammed, telephones jammed or non-functional, facilities may be damaged |
| Communications frequencies adequate for radio traffic | Radio frequencies often overloaded |
| Communications primarily intra-organizational | Need for inter-organizational information sharing |
| Use of familiar terminology in communicating | Communication with persons who use different terminology |
| Need to deal mainly with local press | Hordes of national and international reporters |
| Management structure adequate to coordinate the number of resources involved | Resources often exceed management capacity (e.g. management structure not adequate to coordinate the number of resources involved) |

In the United States, the Stafford Act outlines two types of disaster declarations: emergency declarations and major disaster declarations. While both authorize the president to provide supplemental federal disaster assistance, the event related to the disaster declaration and type and amount of assistance differ.

*Emergency declarations* can be declared for any occasion or instance when the president determines federal assistance is needed. They supplement state and local efforts in providing emergency services, such as the protection of lives, property, public health, and safety, or lessening or averting the threat of a catastrophe in any part of the United States. The total amount of assistance provided for a single emergency may not exceed $5 million. If this amount is exceeded, the president shall report to Congress.

The president declares *major declarations* for a natural event, including any hurricane, tornado, storm, high water, wind-driven water, tidal wave, tsunami, earthquake, volcanic eruption, landslide, mudslide, snowstorm, drought, or, regardless of cause, fire, flood, or explosion, that the president believes has caused damage of such severity that it is beyond the combined capabilities of state and local governments to respond. It provides a wide range of federal assistance programs for individuals and public infrastructure, including funds for both emergency and permanent work.[4]

In Canada, the definition of a disaster has to meet one or more of the following criteria:
- Ten or more people killed
- One hundred or more people affected, injured, infected, evacuated, or homeless
- An appeal made for national or international assistance
- Historical significance
- Significant damage or interruption of normal processes such that the community affected cannot recover on its own[5]

# TYPES OF DISASTERS

## Natural disasters

Most of us are familiar with natural disasters. Specific types of natural disasters include:
- hurricanes, tropical storms, cyclones, and typhoons
- floods and flash floods
- storm surges
- thunderstorms and lightning
- tornadoes
- tsunamis
- volcanic eruptions
- fires and wildfires
- hailstorms
- landslides, avalanches, and mudslides
- agricultural diseases
- drought and water shortage
- earthquakes and sinkholes
- extreme heat
- winter and ice storms

Hurricanes and tropical storms are among the most powerful natural disasters because of their size and destructive potential. Tornadoes are relatively brief but violent, causing winds in excess of 300 kilometers (186 miles) per hour. Both earthquakes and tornadoes strike suddenly without warning.

Flooding is the most common natural hazard and requires an understanding of the natural systems of our environment, including floodplains and the frequency of flooding events. Communities are more vulnerable to wildfires in the event of extreme dry weather.

# Manmade and technological disasters

Humans can also cause disasters. Hazardous materials emergencies can include situations like chemical spills, groundwater contamination, and train explosions. Workplace fires are more common, causing both significant property damage and loss of life.

Increasingly communities are becoming more vulnerable to threats posed by extremist groups that use violence against both people and property. High-risk targets include military and civilian government facilities, international airports, major events, large cities, and high-profile landmarks.

Cyberterrorism involves attacks against computers and networks done to intimidate or coerce a government or its people for political or social reasons.

Specific types of manmade or technological disasters include:
- hazardous materials and chemicals
- building fires or explosions
- power-service disruption or infrastructure failure
- environmental-health concerns
- acts of terrorism
- water or food contamination
- chemical and biological weapons
- plant closures
- industrial or transportation accident
- nuclear power plant emergencies
- radiological threats
- war
- emergency diseases (pandemic influenza or outbreaks)
- civil unrest, disturbances, and riots
- cyberattacks
- fraud and theft

# COST OF DISASTERS

Disasters are increasing in both number and frequency across the world, resulting in ever-growing human suffering and economic cost. On a global scale, the economic cost of the most significant disasters[6] is reported as:

Figure 2. *The Most Costly Disasters*

| Year | Event | Country | Economic Cost ($ Billions) |
|---|---|---|---|
| 2011 | Tōhoku earthquake and tsunami | Japan | $300+ |
| 2017 | Hurricane Harvey | United States | Estimated at over $216 |
| 2008 | Sichuan earthquake | China | $148 |
| 1995 | Great Hanshin earthquake | Japan | $102.5 |
| 2010 | Deepwater Horizon oil spill | United States | $60–100 |
| 2017 | Hurricane Irma | Antigua and Barbuda, Saint Martin, Anguilla, Turks and Caicos, The Bahamas, Cuba, and the United States | $62.9 |
| 2017 | Hurricane Maria | Dominica, Dominican Republic, Guadalupe, Haiti, Martinique, Saint Kitts and Nevis, Puerto Rico, US Virgin Islands, United States | $51.2 |
| 2005 | Hurricane Katrina | United States | $45 (insurance compensated) |
| 2011 | Thailand floods | Thailand | $45.7 (estimate of economic damage/loss) |

| | | | |
|---|---|---|---|
| 2011 | Christchurch earthquake | New Zealand | $40 |
| 2008 | Hurricane Ike | United States | $29.6 |
| 1998 | Yangtze River floods | China | $26 |
| 1992 | Hurricane Andrew | United States | $25 |
| 2001 | September 11 terrorist attacks | United States | $20.7 |
| 1994 | Northridge earthquake | United States | $20 |
| 1986 | Chernobyl disaster | Ukraine | $15 direct loss + future impacts |
| 2004 | Indian Ocean earthquake and tsunami | Indian Ocean | $15 |
| 1985 | Armero tragedy | Columbia | $7 |
| 1989 | Exxon Valdez oil spill | United States | $2.5 (clean up oil spill); $1.1 (recovery for settlements); $2.8 (economic loss due to damages ecosystem) |
| 2016 | Fort McMurray wildfires | Canada | $3.6+ (insurable damage) |
| 2001 | AZF chemical plant explosion | France | $2.1 |
| 2003 | Cedar fire | United States | $2 |
| 1998 | Ice storms | Canada | $1.9 (insurable damage) |
| 2013 | Southern Alberta floods | Canada | $1.8 (insurable damage) |
| 2011 | Slave Lake wildfire | Canada | $750 million |

# NATURE OF DISASTERS

While some disasters such as hurricanes and flooding can provide limited advance warning, other events such as a tornado or terrorist attack provide little to no warning. Many times they catch communities off guard, requiring a high level of coordination among all levels of government to respond to the event.

No country is immune to disasters. Natural and human-induced hazards and disasters are becoming more common in urban and rural communities. Every day the news is reporting another natural disaster somewhere on the planet. Terrorist attacks on Western targets seem to persist. These events can have profound, negative effects on communities.

Accumulating risks associated with factors such as terrorism, animal and human diseases, critical infrastructure interdependencies and dependencies, climate/environmental change, increased urbanization, and increased movement of people and goods around the world have increased the potential for various types of catastrophes. Many of these transcend geographic boundaries and increasingly challenge emergency management response and recovery efforts.

While provincial, state, and federal governments have a significant role in disaster response and recovery, it is important to remember that all disasters are local. They disrupt the physical, social, and economic landscape of neighborhoods, towns, cities, and regions.

# PHASES OF A DISASTER

Emergency management is based on a four-phase model designed to help emergency managers prepare for and respond to disasters. It is also known as the "life cycle" of comprehensive emergency management or the Emergency Management Continuum.

The four priorities of emergency management are to:
- ✓ Save lives and minimize impact on people
- ✓ Protect property
- ✓ Protect the environment
- ✓ Protect the economy

Communities need to coordinate and integrate their prevention and mitigation, preparedness, response, and recovery functions to maximize community safety.

These four phases of emergency management are interdependent components, as seen in Figure 3. While they may be undertaken sequentially or concurrently, they are not independent of each other.

Figure 3. *Emergency Management Continuum*

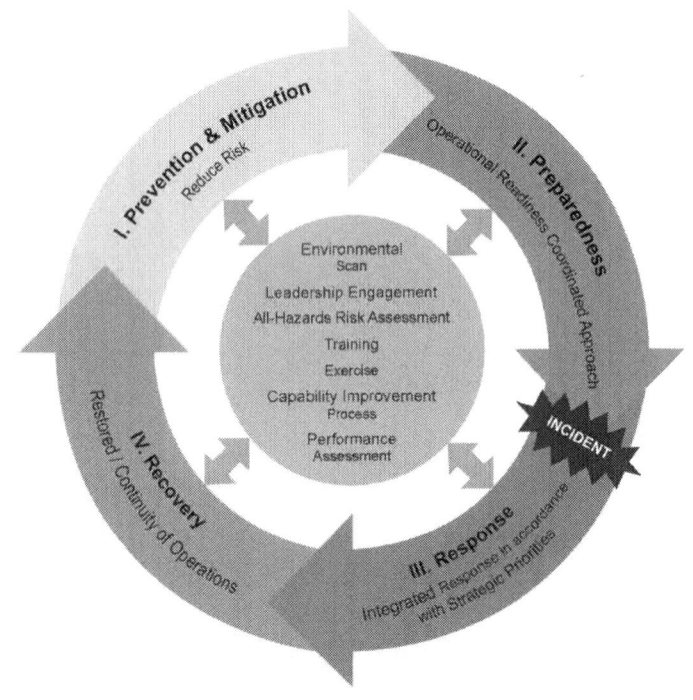

## Prevention and Mitigation

In this phase, the focus is to eliminate or reduce the risk of disasters in order to protect lives, property, and the environment, as well as reduce economic disruption. Prevention and mitigation may be considered independently, or one may include the other.

You can do many things to protect yourself, your business, and your community *before* a disaster hits. This includes identifying your hazards, vulnerabilities, and risks in advance and taking responsibility to mitigate where at all possible.

Mitigation reduces or eliminates risks before a disaster strikes and involves advance planning, preparation, resource mobilization, and communication. It also lessens the potential impact of a disaster on people, property, communities, and an economy.

At a practical level, mitigation efforts could include:
- using fire-retardant materials in homes and buildings for fire mitigation
- changing local building codes or reinforcing walls to fortify homes and buildings for earthquake hazard mitigation
- raising homes, constructing dykes, or changing zoning to forbid development on floodplains and along coastlines for flood mitigation
- mapping community hazards and vulnerabilities
- increasing air emission rules for manufacturing plants
- strengthening public infrastructure to make it more resilient to a catastrophic event

Paying greater attention to and investing in prevention and mitigation can help prevent disasters or at least significantly reduce the social, economic, and environmental costs and damages when events do occur.

## Preparedness

Preparedness is about being ready to respond to a disaster and managing its consequences through measures taken prior to an event.

Capacity building initiatives taken in this phase include activities like:
- Developing emergency response plans
- Providing business continuity training
- Engaging in pre-disaster strategic planning
- Creating resource inventories

- Conducting training and mock exercises
- Striking mutual assistance agreements
- Executing logistical readiness activities
- Implementing public outreach

## Response

The response phase addresses immediate threats presented by the disaster, including saving lives, meeting humanitarian needs (e.g., food, shelter, clothing, public health, and safety), disseminating crisis communications, executing search and rescue, evacuating, cleaning up, assessing damage, and commencing resource distribution.

This somewhat chaotic phase can last a month or more, depending on the nature of the disaster and the extent of the damage. Federal government resources, such as military support (in the case of a major disaster) and nonprofit humanitarian resources such as the Red Cross, Salvation Army, and Samaritans Purse are deployed during this phase.

## Recovery

The recovery process is a sequence of interdependent, often-overlapping activities or phases that progressively advance the community toward a successful recovery. Decisions a community makes, and the priorities it sets early on in the recovery process can have a cascading effect on the nature and speed of the overall recovery process. Response and short-term recovery functions occur simultaneously. There is no finite date between phases. The transition to intermediate- and long-term recovery occurs as immediate response activities wind down.

*Short-term recovery* refers to the first days and weeks after the incident. This phase addresses health and safety needs beyond rescue, assessment of the scope of damage and needs, restoration of basic infrastructure, activation of recovery organizations, and mobilization of resources.

*Intermediate recovery* refers to the weeks and months after the incident. This phase involves returning individuals, families, critical infrastructure, and essential government or commercial services to a functional, if not pre-disaster state.

*Long-term recovery* refers to the months and years after the incident. This phase addresses complete redevelopment and revitalization of the impacted area; rebuilding or relocating of damaged or destroyed social, economic, natural, and built environments; and a move to self-sufficiency, sustainability, and resilience.

It is important to understand that long-term recovery can take years, even with effective strategic management processes in place. Depending on the nature of the disaster, sometimes it can even take decades.

There is a strong relationship between long-term sustainable recovery, prevention, and mitigation of future disasters. Recovery efforts should always be conducted with a view toward disaster risk reduction.

The following recovery continuum[8] in Figure 4 illustrates the recovery process from pre-incident to the long-term.

Figure 4. Recovery Continuum

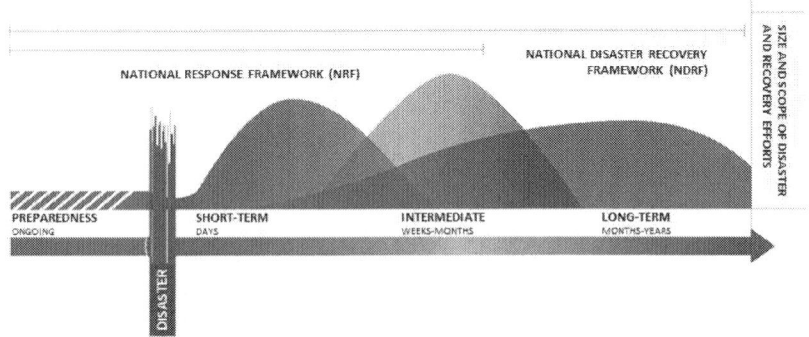

PRE-DISASTER PREPAREDNESS

- *Pre-disaster recovery planning*
- *Mitigation planning and implementation*
- *Community capacity and resilience-building*
- *Conducting disaster preparedness exercises*
- *Partnership building*
- *Articulate protocols in disaster plans for services to meet emotional and health care needs of adults and children*

SHORT-TERM RECOVERY

- *Integrate mass care and emergency services*
- *Clear debris from major transportation routes*
- *Establish temporary or interim infrastructure to help businesses reopen, re-establish cash flow*
- *Identify adults and children that need mental health supports*
- *Provide emergency and temporary medical care and establish appropriate surveillance protocols*
- *Mitigation activities, assess and understand risks and vulnerabilities*

### INTERMEDIATE RECOVERY

- *Provide accessible interim housing solutions*
- *Initiate debris removal*
- *Immediate infrastructure repair and restoration*
- *Support reestablishment of businesses where appropriate*
- *Support establishment of a business recovery center*
- *Engage support networks for ongoing care*
- *Ensure continuity of care through temporary facilities*
- *Inform community members of opportunities to build back stronger*

### LONG-TERM RECOVERY

- *Develop permanent housing solutions*
- *Rebuild infrastructure to meet future community needs*
- *Implement economic revitalization strategies*
- *Facilitate funding to business rebuilding*
- *Follow-up for ongoing counseling, behavioral health, and case management services*
- *Re-establish disrupted health care facilities*
- *Implement mitigation strategies*

# BUSINESS MODULE

Small- and medium-sized businesses have strong roots in a local economy and are often more vulnerable to disasters than large businesses.

Most small businesses underestimate the likelihood and impact of a major crisis on their business. Yet when disaster strikes, a number of these businesses could lose their customer base, property, inventory, and sales records in a single day. According to KPMG, 40 percent of companies that suffer a major business disruption go out of business within two years.[9]

While most small- to medium-sized business owners are focused on trying to make payroll for the month, planning for disaster tends to fall by the wayside. It's on the to-do list when things slow down. For those who have actually operated a small business, you know that things rarely slow down.

Depending on the nature and magnitude of the disaster, a business owner may have very little time to react and respond. Therefore, developing a plan helps protect your business investment and gives your company a better chance for survival. You can also help limit employee injuries, decrease property damage, and return to normal operations more quickly.

All businesses should have a formal business continuity plan that describes a clear set of actions for the business and its employees to follow in order to restore its core business functions after a disaster.

Continuity planning should also account for both manmade and natural disasters.

Be prepared to assess various situations, use common sense, and access available resources to take care of yourself, your coworkers, and your overall business recovery.

What would happen if your facility burned to the ground or was flooded? Would your landlord continue to charge rent? Would your inventory be covered? Would you be able to continue to employ your workers? Do you have enough cash in your bank account to float you for six months if you are unable to access your place of work?

Business preparedness yields a number of practical benefits regardless of where it is located or what level of risk it faces:[10]

- It enhances a company's ability to recover from financial or market share losses, repair damages to equipment or products, and minimize business interruption.
- It facilitates compliance with regulatory safety requirements of federal, state/provincial, and local agencies.
- It helps companies fulfill their responsibility to protect its employees, the community, and the environment.
- It bolsters a company's security and enhances its credibility with employees, customers, suppliers, and the community.
- It can help reduce insurance costs.

When it comes to your business, if you want to continue operating your business in a post-disaster environment, you need to learn how to *Master Your Disaster* before it happens.

This module has been developed to help you:
- ✓ Assess and mitigate your risks
- ✓ Plan and practice your response
- ✓ Activate your plan
- ✓ Recover successfully
- ✓ Template your activity in advance

# ASSESS AND MITIGATE YOUR RISKS

What types of disasters are most likely to impact your business? Do they pose a low or high risk to your business? Would the impact be minimal or significant? What type of disaster would they be?

It is helpful to understand which disasters are most common in the areas where you operate. You may be aware of some, but others may surprise you.

**Security**: theft, vandalism, fraud, cyberattacks, software/hardware failure

**Natural disasters**: flood, hurricane, hail, tornado, earthquake, severe winter weather, wildfire

**Staffing and operations**: labor unrest, loss/illness of staff, major pandemic, supply chain disruptions, workplace violence

**Manmade**: chemical spill, utility or telecommunications disruption, factory fire, power outage, loss of premises

Then, in assessing the various types of risks, it is important to determine how they could affect your ability to maintain normal operations and mitigate the impact.

The specific industry, size, and scope of your business will determine your overall risk assessment needs. Utilizing the risk matrix assessment tool in Template #1 can be helpful for this exercise.

# Identify critical business functions

It is also important to identify critical business functions in advance.

There are a number of templates and resources to help with this, but the Institute for Business and Home Safety has produced one of the most helpful checklists.[11]

First ask yourself:
- ✓ What are my most critical, time-sensitive business functions?
- ✓ Which functions would I classify as high priority? Medium priority? Low priority?
- ✓ How much downtime can I tolerate for each function?
- ✓ Which functions are necessary to fulfill my legal and financial obligations and maintain cash flow?
- ✓ Which functions are critical to maintain my market share and reputation or need to be adjusted due to changed circumstances?

Then determine how critical each function is:
- ✓ What is my organization's core business?
- ✓ What would the consequences be if I lost or did not have access to my:
    - o Facilities/buildings
    - o Contents/inventory
    - o People (employees or customers)
    - o Vital records
    - o Equipment
    - o Utilities
    - o Support systems (e.g., computers, networks, communications, and transportation)
    - o Suppliers

# Understand your insurance plan

Every business owner should review his or her insurance coverage yearly to make sure he or she has appropriate coverage in terms of replacement costs for the business, as well as business interruption insurance for different types of hazards.

Perhaps the most common issue facing businesses after a disaster is to understand what their insurance policy does and does not cover. Insurance policies are extremely difficult to understand. Make sure you review your commercial policy on a regular basis with your insurance broker so you know what types of coverage there is for your type of business and what type of coverage you have.

While you may not like incurring this cost of doing business, it could be the one thing that actually saves your business in the long term. Having adequate insurance in place is a smart investment and wise business decision.

When doing your annual insurance review with your broker, consider the following questions:
- Is your business located in an area that is particularly vulnerable to specific hazards such as flooding, tornadoes, forest fires, earthquakes, or hurricanes? What does that mean for your insurance coverage?
- Do you need to buy additional insurance coverage? Most commercial property insurance does not cover flood or windstorm damage. Overland flood insurance may be available for businesses, excluding those operating out of the home.
- Do you have business interruption insurance? Know what is and is not covered.

- Did you look for the cheapest insurance policy? Beware of companies that offer a lowball bid where the quote comes in significantly lower than other rates. This may either be a stripped-down service or subject to a significant rate increase when the insurance policy comes up for renewal. You do get what you pay for.
- Has your business grown recently? If so, you may need to review liabilities in terms of expanded equipment or operations. Are you covered for a sufficient amount to rebuild the structure of your operation or replace fixtures at current replacement prices? After a disaster, you will not be in a position to shop around for good prices as supplies will be short. It is much smarter to overestimate replacement costs.
- Do you have cyber liability insurance to protect you from the threat of cyberattacks? This is a growing concern for many businesses. Make sure you inquire about whether this coverage is available or recommended.

## PLAN AND PRACTICE YOUR RESPONSE

Developing a plan when there is no impending crisis is the best way to ensure your operations will continue both during and after a crisis.

Do not develop a plan just to have it sit on a shelf. It should be tested, refined, and updated on a regular basis. Management must be committed to the plan, or it won't receive the importance and buy-in it requires.

The Institute for Business & Home Safety produces an Open for Business® disaster protection and recovery planning toolkit for small- to midsized businesses.[12]

It is a comprehensive planning tool designed to help protect companies, their employees, and customers from a disaster loss. Template #1 is also included at the end of this module to start templating your own business continuity plan.

## Assemble an emergency business supply kit

All employees should be encouraged to have emergency preparedness kits at home and in their vehicles if possible.

It is also important for businesses to have a disaster response kit available in the case of an emergency.

Types of items to include in your kit include:
- first aid kit
- emergency contact list (including staff numbers)
- important records (as outlined earlier)
- cash and ATM/credit card(s)
- local maps
- battery-powered or hand crank radio with extra batteries
- wind-up flashlights and light sticks
- whistle
- non-perishable food, utensils, and paper supplies
- manual can opener
- plastic bags
- basic tools (e.g., screwdriver, hammer, etc.)
- bottled water in non-breakable containers
- dust mask to filter contaminated air, hand sanitizer, and rubber gloves
- blankets

# Develop evacuation procedures and identify routes

- How does your emergency notification system work?
- If there were an impending threat, how would you know? Would it be through an online emergency alert system? Or would it be through the radio or TV?
- How will you notify employees?
- If you need to evacuate your building, where are your emergency exits?
- What route do you use?
- Do all employees know the route?
- Where are your primary and secondary muster points?

All of these questions should be considered when developing your evacuation procedures and establishing primary and secondary evacuation routes.

# Identify an alternate office location

As part of your business continuity plan, you should plan for at least one backup office location, preferably two, to use in the case of an emergency or disaster. This helps ensure that, if the primary location is impacted, a secondary location is available.

- Where will you operate if you are unable to go back to your regular place of business for a period of time?
- What if your street, community, or region is not accessible for a week or month?
- Do you have protocols in place to enable your staff to work remotely?
- Can you borrow equipment from another business or use old equipment?

## Consider employees

Prepare for the unexpected. Having a robust employee communication plan in place is particularly important if the disaster happens outside of normal operation hours or on the weekend.

- Does your disaster plan take into account the needs of your employees, including their safety and well-being, in the event of a major disaster?
- If a disaster happens during normal hours of operation, do you have emergency contact information for your employees so you can notify their families if the disaster makes it difficult for them to leave the work premises?
- Do you have current contact details for all of your employees, including home and personal cell phone numbers and email addresses? Depending on the magnitude and impact of the disaster, they will need to be informed of the status of your business operations, where, when, and if they should report to work.

Senior management must be cautious and sensitive in communicating with employees during this time as they are often your most key assets to protect and serve. Employees may be experiencing damage to their homes, closure of daycare and schools, transportation challenges, or potential injury or death of family members and friends.

Consider various communications channels in case the phone system is not working, internet access is unavailable, or an extended power outage occurs.

Large companies should consider setting up a special number for employees to call into or forwarding their main business line. Securing a number outside of your region or area code can increase the probability of communication if the disaster is significant. Often local phone lines are overloaded with people trying to find out if their family and friends are OK.

Business owners should also consider include sending emails to an employee's work and personal addresses as well as posting information on the company website.

Meet with your employees at least once a year to review emergency plans and update emergency contact details. Plan and practice various scenarios. Make sure you have strategies in place for each one. Update the plan as required.

## Ensure important records are safe

All businesses rely on access to data. At a minimum, companies should keep copies of important records and other priority documents in a waterproof, fireproof portable container. A second set of records should be stored at an off-site location.

Types of information to be stored include:
- employee identification and emergency contact information
- site maps, building plans, or blueprints
- a copy of your lease
- commercial insurance policy
- bank account information
- most recent tax filing
- customer, vendor, and shipping contact lists
- computer backups of vital records (e.g., payroll, financial records, load documents, strategic plans, corporate policies and procedures, and contracts)
- emergency or law enforcement contact numbers

**Consider cybersecurity measures**

Cyberattacks are on the rise, and increasingly small businesses are being targeted. The most common cyberattacks are socially engineered malware, password phishing attacks, unpatched software, social media threats, and advanced persistent threats to steal intellectual property.[13]

These incidents can have a significant business impact. Some of the most common impacts include:
- operational disruption
- customer breach notifications
- post-breach customer protection
- regulatory compliance (fines)
- public relations/crises communications
- legal fees and litigation
- cybersecurity improvements
- technical investigations
- increases to insurance premiums
- increased cost to raise debt
- lost value of customer relationships
- value of lost contract revenue
- devaluation of trade name
- loss of intellectual property[14]

In today's connected, global world, businesses should not ignore their risk of a cyberattack, and develop a plan for this inevitability. Start by identifying your most important information and understand where it resides. Actively monitor access to the data across various networks, systems, and endpoint devices.

**Basic tips on cybersecurity**

- Keep data out of the hands of unauthorized users. Practice "clean desk" and "put away" policies to keep sensitive information away from them.
- Lock up sensitive data.
- Restrict data access to those who have a "need to know."
- Put security systems in place, and ensure all visitors sign in.
- Record and regularly review your data practices and retrain staff when changes are made.[15]

**Managing your technology**

- Conduct routine audits to ensure policies you have in place are working to protect data.
- Limit the use of portable technology when dealing with sensitive information and ensure remote network access is secure.
- Don't use unsecured wireless networks, as they do not provide adequate enterprise-level security to protect data.
- Install antivirus, anti-spyware, and firewalls. To maintain the most up-to-date protection, download system and security patches, antivirus, and anti-malware updates.
- Review and consider any and all access outside contractors or vendors have to sensitive data and determine the need for it.
- Properly dispose of sensitive data. Implement policies on how to securely destroy any technology hardware that may contain sensitive information. Similar practices should be used to properly dispose of sensitive data that is paper-based.[16]

# Identify critical business processes

- Do you have unique business needs or resources?
- If the power went out, would your inventory be at high risk of loss?
- Is your business critical during the response phase?
- Is access to your property a priority over other businesses?
- Do you have equipment and resources that could be helpful in a state of emergency?

If you answer yes to any of these questions, working with your local emergency operations center prior to a disaster would probably be a worthwhile exercise.

Normally we think *critical* is life threatening. This definition is good when we are planning for a disaster, as we want our business to survive. When examining each process or function, it is helpful to consider whether your business can survive without it.

- **Is it vital?** These functions usually cannot be performed manually. If they are, it is for only a very brief period of time. They will require a considerable amount of time to restore.
- **Is it sensitive?** These processes can be performed manually with difficulty but at a tolerable cost for an extended period of time. They will require catching up once restored.
- **Is it noncritical?** These processes may be interrupted for an extended period of time at little or no cost to the company and require little or no catching up once restored.

## Rank critical business processes

How long would it take to get your business back to normal after a disruption? What would need to be recovered immediately? How long could you go without power before you would compromise your business?

One way to better understand the criticality of each business function is to look at a recovery time objective (RTO).

An RTO refers to the targeted duration of time and service level within which a business process must be restored after a disruption in order to avoid unacceptable consequences. The following chart is an example of how you can categorize RTOs. It allows you to better understand which business functions are critical to your recovery and at what point.

Figure 5. *Recovery Time Objectives (RTO)*

| Business Function | \<24 Hours | \<48 Hours | \<72 Hours | 1 Week | 2 Weeks | 1 Month |
|---|---|---|---|---|---|---|
| Payroll | | | | | | X |
| Sales | | | | | X | |
| Production | | | | | | X |
| Delivery | | | | | | X |

# Develop strategies to address risks

Based on your assessed risk and recovery time objectives (RTO), you can then take each risk and develop a desired action plan around it.

This is where it becomes important to identify strategies you can implement before, during, and after a disruption occurs.

Figure 6. *Risk Action Plan*

| Potential Risk | |
|---|---|
| Risk Level | |
| RTO | |
| Business Function(s) Affected | |
| Potential Impact(s) | |
| Actions — Before | |
| Actions — During | |
| Actions — After | |
| Staff Required | |
| Resources Required | |

# Create a crisis communication plan

It is important to develop your crisis communication plan in advance of a disaster. Having clear roles, responsibilities, and messages prepared in advance will help you manage and recover from the crisis much more effectively.

- In addition to having an internal communication plan developed for employees, what is your plan to communicate externally with suppliers and customers?
- Do you have their emergency numbers in a safe place? Are they up to date?
- Who will be the key spokesperson for your business?
- What messages do you want to convey?
- When should you convey them?
- What do your various audiences need to know?
- Do you have templates ready to go if a disaster hits tomorrow?

- What social media platforms will you utilize?
- What channels will you use if internet and phone lines are unavailable?

All these questions should be considered as you develop, test, refine, and practice your ongoing crisis communication planning efforts.

# ACTIVATE YOUR BUSINESS CONTINUITY PLAN

When and if it comes time to activate your plan, be confident your advance planning and practice efforts will help minimize potential impacts.

Once you and your employees are in a safe place, you can commence your response, recovery, and restoration efforts.

- **Assess the type and extent of the incident.** What happened? When? What caused it? How are authorities responding? When can you get access to your building to see what happened? Are there any security issues? How can you avoid more damage?
- **Manage the incident.** Gather resources, prepare an alternate site if needed, and activate critical business functions/procedures.
- **Notify employees.** Communicate with your employees as soon as possible so they understand if and when they can continue working. Let them know what happened and what you want them to do in the short term (e.g., stay at home, work remotely, apply for unemployment insurance, etc.) as well as when they will get paid.

# RECOVER FROM THE INCIDENT

Once you have resumed operations and recovered your critical business functions, you can take steps to fully restore your business. This may include returning to a damaged property, dealing with significant clean up, disposing of damaged inventory, restoring technology infrastructure, and filing insurance claims.

# UPDATE YOUR PLAN

To be successful when and if a business disruption occurs, you need to continue to maintain, and update your plan on a regular basis.

For example, every six months a business should ask its employees to review the plan and consider the following questions:

- Is anything out of date?
- Is all of the contact information up to date?
- Have any procedures changed?
- Have there been any changes in business priorities?
- Have any responsibilities changed?

Once the plan is reviewed and updated, it is important to test the plan with your key employees to ensure they know what to do in case the plan needs activated in the future.

Template #1 is a great resource to use in developing your own business continuity plan.

# TEMPLATE #1: STAND APART©
# BUSINESS CONTINUITY PLAN

Use the following template to develop and periodically update your Business Continuity Plan.

## GENERAL BUSINESS INFORMATION

>Name
>Street Address
>City, Province/State
>Postal/Zip

## EMERGENCY PLANNING TEAM

- The following people will participate in emergency planning and crisis management: (Note: List them all.)
- The following people from neighboring businesses and our building management will participate on our emergency planning team: (Note: List them all.)

## CRISIS MANAGERS

*Primary Crisis Manager*

>Name
>Work Number
>Cell Number
>Home Number
>Email Address

***Alternate Crisis Manager*** *(if Primary Unavailable)*

    Name
    Work Number
    Cell Number
    Home Number
    Email Address

## IMPORTANT NUMBERS OR INFORMATION

    Police
    Fire
    Poison Control
    Health Benefits (Provider and Policy Number)
    Nearest Hospital/Clinic
    Commercial Insurance (Provider and Policy Number)
    Electric Company
    Gas Company
    Water Company
    Other

## ASSESS AND MITIGATE RISKS

## RISK MATRIX

It is important to identify potential risks to our business, rank the probability and severity of each, and understand the impact they could have on various business functions.

## TYPES OF RISKS

- *Security:* theft, vandalism, fraud, cyberattacks, software/hardware failure
- *Natural disasters:* flood, hurricane, hail, tornado, earthquake, severe winter weather, wildfire
- *Staffing and operations:* labor unrest, loss/illness of staff, major pandemic, supply chain disruption, workplace violence
- *Manmade:* chemical spill, utility or telecommunications disruption, factory fire, power outage, loss of premises

The following risk matrix identifies and ranks various threats to our business operations:

| Probability \ Impact | Minor | Moderate | Major | Extreme |
|---|---|---|---|---|
| Rare | Low | Low | Medium | Medium |
| Unlikely | Low | Medium | Medium | Medium |
| Moderate | Medium | Medium | Medium | High |
| Likely | Medium | Medium | High | High |
| Very Likely | Medium | High | High | High |

| Likelihood (Probability) | Consequences (Impact) |
|---|---|
| 5. Almost certain | 5. Fatality |
| 4. Probable | 4. Major injury resulting in disability |
| 3. Possible | 3. Injury requires doctor's or hospital attendance |
| 2. Possible (under unfortunate circumstances) | 2. Minor injury, first aid required |
| 1. Rare | 1. Minor injury, first aid not required |

# IDENTIFY AND RANK CRITICAL BUSINESS FUNCTIONS OR OPERATIONS

We also need to think about the activities our employees perform on a daily, weekly, monthly, and annual basis. What functions and processes are required to run our finance, production, service delivery, sales, marketing, customer service, human resources, administration, information technology, and purchasing?

The following is a prioritized list of our critical business operations, including the staff, and procedures required to recover from a disaster:

| Function/ Operation | Priority (Extremely high, high, medium, low) | Staff Requirements (Who is in charge?) | Action Plan (Resource requirements to perform function) | How to complete function (Including workaround methods) |
|---|---|---|---|---|
|  |  |  |  |  |
|  |  |  |  |  |
|  |  |  |  |  |
|  |  |  |  |  |

The table below provides our recovery time objective (RTO) for each business function. By ranking them this way, we can see which ones are most critical to our recovery.

| Recovery Time Objective (RTO) ||||||| 
| Business Function | <24 Hours | <48 Hours | <72 Hours | 1 Week | 2 Weeks | 1 Month |
|---|---|---|---|---|---|---|
| Payroll |  |  |  |  |  | X |
| Sales |  |  |  |  | X |  |
| Production |  |  |  |  |  | X |
| Delivery |  |  |  |  |  | X |

## DEVELOP OUR RISK ACTION PLAN

Based on our business RTOs, our plan to mitigate each risk is as follows:

| | | |
|---|---|---|
| **Potential Risk** | | |
| **Risk Level** | | |
| **RTO** | | |
| **Business Function(s) Affected** | | |
| **Potential Impact(s)** | | |
| **Actions** | Before | |
| | During | |
| | After | |
| **Staff Required** | | |
| **Resources Required** | | |

## PLAN AND PRACTICE OUR RESPONSE

### EMERGENCY KIT

- Who is responsible to assemble and maintain our emergency business supply kit?
- Who is responsible to bring the emergency business supply kit if we are evacuated?
- We have talked to co-workers about which emergency supplies the company will provide in the shelter location and which supplies they should consider keeping in a portable kit personalized for their individual needs. **Yes   No**

## SHELTER-IN-PLACE PLAN FOR *(Insert Address)*

- How many times will we practice shelter procedures each year?
- How many times will we test the warning system and record results annually?
- Storm shelter location:
- Seal the room shelter location:
- Shelter manager name:
- Shelter manager alternate:
- Shelter manager responsibilities:
- Shut-down manager name:
- Shut-down manager alternate:
- Shut-down manager responsibilities:

## EVACUATION PLAN FOR *(Insert Address)*

- We have developed our plans in collaboration with neighboring businesses and building owners to avoid confusion or gridlock. **Yes   No**
- We have located, copied, and posted building and site maps. **Yes   No**
- Exits are clearly marked. **Yes   No**
- How many times will we practice evacuation procedures each year?
- If we must leave the workplace quickly, we will go to:
- How many times each year will we test the warning system and record results?
- Where will we assemble upon evacuation?
- Who is responsible for issuing the all clear?

## ALTERNATE LOCATION

- If our location is not accessible, we will operate from:
    Business Name
    Address
    Phone Number

## INFORMATION TECHNOLOGY

- If our computers are destroyed, we will use back-up computers at the following location:
- Information about our computer equipment/hardware is as follows: (e.g., serial numbers, registered user names, purchase/lease information, technical support number, primary supplier)
- To protect our computer hardware, we will:
- Information about our computer software is as follows: (e.g. number of licenses, license numbers, version number)
- To protect our computer software, we will:
- The person responsible for backing up our critical records, including payroll and accounting systems is:
- If our accounting and payroll records are destroyed, we will provide for continuity in the following ways:
- Back-up records, including a copy of this plan, site maps, insurance policies, bank account records, and computer backups, are stored at the following location:
- Another set of back-up records is stored at this off-site location:

## FINANCES

- Do we have an emergency cash reserve fund to purchase supplies, equipment or to relocate the business? How much cash would we require to survive a shutdown?
- Will we have access to a line of credit or credit card if we don't have enough emergency cash?
- What financial obligations or expenses will need to be paid even if a disaster strikes?
- Will we be able to continue to accept payments from customers for accounts receivable?
- Do we have a payroll continuity plan in place for employees? Are our employees aware of payroll policies that will be in place during a disruption?

- Do we have adequate insurance in place? Do we understand our coverage, deductibles, limits, and how to file a claim?

**COMMUNICATION**

- Our key spokesperson for the company is:
- Our alternate, if the key spokesperson is unavailable is:
- Our key messages to convey are:
- We have communication templates prepared in advance. Templates could include press releases, news releases, employee email templates, social media updates etc.:
- We will communicate our emergency plans with co-workers in the following way:

In the event of a disaster, we will communicate with employees in the following way:

| Name | Position | Role/ Responsibility | Home Number | Cell Number | Address | (First Aid, CRP, EMT, Ham Radio etc.) |
|------|----------|----------------------|-------------|-------------|---------|----------------------------------------|
|      |          |                      |             |             |         |                                        |
|      |          |                      |             |             |         |                                        |

In the event of a disaster, we will communicate with our customers, suppliers, and vendors in the following way:

| Company | Contact | Complete Mailing Address | Phone Number | Email Address | Account Number | Product/ Service Provided |
|---------|---------|--------------------------|--------------|---------------|----------------|---------------------------|
|         |         |                          |              |               |                |                           |
|         |         |                          |              |               |                |                           |

If our regular supplier(s) are unavailable or unable to provide products or services, our alternate supplier(s) are:

| Company | Contact | Complete Mailing Address | Phone Number | Email | Address | Account Number | Service Provided |
|---------|---------|--------------------------|--------------|-------|---------|----------------|------------------|
|         |         |                          |              |       |         |                |                  |
|         |         |                          |              |       |         |                |                  |

## ACTIVATE OUR BUSINESS CONTINUITY PLAN

- In the case of an emergency or disaster, we will activate our business continuity plan as approved
- Once our employees are safe we will:
    - Assess the type and extent of the incident
    - Manage the incident
    - Notify our employees

## RECOVER FROM THE INCIDENT

- Once we have resumed operations and recovered our critical business functions, we will begin to fully restore our business. This includes fixing damaged property, cleaning up our site, disposing of damaged inventory, restoring technology infrastructure, and filing insurance claims.

## TEMPLATE OUR ACTIVITY

- Is all of our contact information up to date?
- Have any procedures or priorities changed?
- Have any roles or responsibilities changed?
- When will the next update of our plan take place?

List of revisions:

| Revision Number | Details | Revised by | Revision Date |
|---|---|---|---|
|  |  |  |  |
|  |  |  |  |
|  |  |  |  |

The following individuals need to have copies of the most current business continuity plan:

| Name | Details | Date |
|---|---|---|
|  |  |  |
|  |  |  |
|  |  |  |

# CONCLUSION

The *Sendai Framework for Disaster Risk Reduction 2015-2030* is a voluntary, nonbinding agreement that recognizes the state has the primary role to reduce disaster risk. However, that responsibility needs to be shared with other stakeholders, including local government, the private sector, and others.

It outlines four priority areas:
- Understanding disaster risk
- Strengthening disaster risk governance to manage disaster risk
- Investing in disaster risk reduction for resilience
- Enhancing disaster preparedness for effective response and to "build back better" in recovery, rehabilitation, and reconstruction[17]

National governments; local government associations; international, regional, and civil society organizations; donors; the private sector; academia; and professional associations as well as every citizen needs to be engaged in risk reduction. It could mean the difference between saving our own life, keeping our livelihood in place, or maintaining our community's quality of life.

Better access to tools, information, and resources can empower us to take the lead on our own response and recovery efforts. Governments, emergency response organizations, and humanitarian relief agencies cannot do it alone. As global citizens, in increasingly challenging times, we have to take an active part in shaping our own destinies.

This guidebook is a first step towards empowerment. It provides an easy, practical way for you to Stand APART© by:
- ✓ **A**ssessing and mitigating your risk
- ✓ **P**lanning and practicing your response
- ✓ **A**ctivating your plan
- ✓ **R**ecovering successfully from the incident
- ✓ **T**emplating your activity in an easy-to-use format

No one knows what tomorrow holds, but we can better prepare our families, businesses and communities for the worst.

I hope as you complete the various Master Your Disaster templates you will have more confidence to act calmly and efficiently when the time comes. Your new foundation in emergency preparedness will make the chaos more controllable—and survivable.

Don't wait—the time is now!

## ABOUT THE AUTHOR

Leann Hackman-Carty has spent nearly thirty years encouraging community economic development, business and economic recovery, and entrepreneurship. Her leadership was recognized on an international level when she was invited to participate in the US International Visitors Program with delegates from nineteen other countries.

Hackman-Carty is currently CEO of Economic Developers Alberta, which works closely with the International Economic Development Council (IEDC) in Washington, DC. In 2014, she helped flooded communities in southern Alberta recover from disaster and develop better resilience. In 2016, she played an active role in Fort McMurray's post-wildfire business and economic recovery efforts. She also helped customize the IEDC's economic recovery and resiliency toolkit for Canadian communities.

Hackman-Carty holds bachelor's degrees in political science/sociology and social work and has earned certificates in both marketing and economic development. She has also received numerous awards for her work in economic development and recovery.

Hackman-Carty lives with her husband, two children, and dog in Calgary, Canada. In her free time, she enjoys traveling and learning about other cultures.

Other *Master Your Disaster* editions available for purchase:
- *Full Edition (English, Spanish and audiobook)*
- *Family Edition*
- *Community Edition*

# TABLE OF FIGURES

Figure 1. *Emergencies vs. Disasters* ................................................................. 2

Figure 2. *The Most Costly Disasters* ................................................................. 6

Figure 3. *Emergency Management Continuum* ........................... 10

Figure 4. *Recovery Continuum* ......................................................... 14

Figure 5. *Recovery Time Objectives (RTO)* .................................... 29

Figure 6. *Risk Action Plan* .................................................................. 30

# REFERENCES

[1] United Nations Office for Outer Space Affairs, http://www.un-spider.org/risks-and-disasters/emergency-and-disaster-management.
[2] "International Federation of Red Cross and Red Crescent Societies," http://www.ifrc.org/en/what-we-do/disaster-management/about-disasters/what-is-a-disaster/.
[3] Alberta Emergency Management Agency, "Basic Emergency Management Manual", page 6.
[4] "Federal Emergency Management Agency," https://www.fema.gov/disaster-declaration-process.
[5] "Public Safety Canada," https://www.publicsafety.gc.ca/cnt/rsrcs/cndn-dsstr-dtbs/index-en.aspx.
[6] "Wikipedia," https://en.wikipedia.org/wiki/List_of_disasters_by_cost.
[7] "Public Safety Canada," https://www.publicsafety.gc.ca/cnt/rsrcs/pblctns/mrgnc-mngmnt-pnnng/index-en.aspx#figure_1.
[8] FEMA Recovery Continuum, "National Disaster Recovery Framework", page 5 (June 2016).
[9] Felipe Alonso, Risk and Advisory Services, KPMG, "Managing Business Continuity Part 1" (2000)."
[10] FEMA "Ready Business Mentoring Guide," http://www.fema.gov/media-library-data/1392217307183-56ed30008abd809cac1a3027488a4c24/2014_business_user_guide.pdf.
[11] Adapted from IBHS "OFB-EZ® (Open for Business-EZ)" stay open for business toolkit, http://disastersafety.org/wp-content/uploads/OFB-EZ_Toolkit_IBHS.pdf.
[12] "IBHS "OFB-EZ® (Open for Business-EZ)" business toolkit, http://www.disastersafety.org/wp-content/uploads/open-for-business-english.pdf.

[13] "The 5 cyber-attacks you're most likely to face," http://www.csoonline.com/article/2616316/data-protection/security-the-5-cyber-attacks-you-re-most-likely-to-face.html#tk.csoendnote.

[14] "A deeper look at business impact of a cyberattack," .http://www.csoonline.com/article/3110756/data-breach/a-deeper-look-at-business-impact-of-a-cyberattack.html.

[15] "Cyber Risks," http://www.insuranceisevolving.com/en/cyber-risk-alberta.html.

[16] Ibid.

[17] "Sendai Framework for Disaster Risk Reduction 2015-2030," http://www.preventionweb.net/files/43291_sendaiframeworkfordrren.pdf.

Manufactured by Amazon.ca
Bolton, ON